COURTNEY CONRAD

I AM EVIDENCE

T0023989

'Courtney Conrad is one of the most promising voices to emerge in the British literary world. A voice of affirmation, testimony, survival and revival. The Jamaican spirit of remixing and mashing up English into new and deeper coherences. These poems are evidence of a truth-telling lyrical arrival.' – RAYMOND ANTROBUS

'These are poems of archive, place and survival which are as bold as they are earnest and insistent on telling the stories of lives often relegated to the domain of footnote, headline and or stereotype.[...] *I Am Evidence* is a remarkable debut on its own terms that will stick with readers long after the last page.' – TOLU AGBELUSI

'Conrad is forging her own distinctive Jamaican poetic seeped in a literary orality, which enables the witness bearing of: the persevered, the forsaken, the rock bottom, the hold on better must come, all speaking to a fragile existence. Yet these are not downtrodden but celebrated as resilient. Conrad continues the tradition of Jamaican poets like Louise Bennett, Jean 'Binta' Breeze and Olive Senior who unapologetically empowered the working-class voice.'
– MALIKA BOOKER

'*I Am Evidence* employs the poetics of witness to lay bare injustice, poverty and violence with an ease of expression and imagery that is fierce and agile. And yet, there is humour, and hope, and joy, in the language, in the celebration of patois that threads the poems.' – DR KEITH JARRETT

'Courtney Conrad is one of the most dynamic and exciting poets I've read in a long, long time. With its striking title alone, Courtney Conrad's debut pamphlet makes a bold, declarative statement. [...] her images blissfully efficient and cinematic. Commanding, witty, bracingly political yet never didactic, *I Am Evidence* engages the voice, the body and the intellect in equal measure.' – VANESSA KISSULE

'Courtney Conrad is an exceptional writer. Her poems are utterly alive and completely immersive; they draw you in and leave you breathless. Each poem is a vivid and expertly drawn world which manages to confront and contain so much. These poems are full of struggle but they simmer with vibrance, with beauty, with truth, with care and with an addictive and distinctive voice.' – CECILIA KNAPP

'Courtney Conrad, what an outstanding, original voice! These poems bear (unbearable) testimony and witness. This is work so rooted and yet transportive, utterly transformative.'
– RACHEL LONG

'Courtney Conrad is an important voice to watch. Her book *I Am Evidence* feels like a new shot in the Caribbean Artist Movement. Throughout the book her identity and culture resonate in the fresh use of national language which enables a nuanced unspooling of hidden Caribbean narratives exploring the micro of Jamaica's underclass as it alludes to the macro of Jamaican politics.' – ROGER ROBINSON

COURTNEY CONRAD

I AM EVIDENCE

BLOODAXE BOOKS

ISBN: 978 1 78037 656 1

First published 2023 by
Bloodaxe Books Ltd,
Eastburn,
South Park,
Hexham,
Northumberland NE46 1BS
in association with *Mslexia*

www.bloodaxebooks.com
For further information about Bloodaxe titles
please visit our website and join our mailing list
or write to the above address for a catalogue

Supported using public funding by
**ARTS COUNCIL
ENGLAND**

Cover design: Neil Astley & Pamela Robertson-Pearce.

Digital reprint of the 2023 Bloodaxe Books edition.

For the glory of God

CONTENTS

Mommy Carry Mi Guh Coronation Market

Saturday mornings, I fish underneath the kitchen sink for crocus bags. Mommy empties her handbag and tucks cash into the lining. We bare our earlobes, necks, and wrists. In the front seat, I scribble a shopping list on the light bill. Coronation Market: rusty iron with patch paintings of the sky. Tarpaulins advertise cassavas, yams and pumpkins. Wire hangers dangle crisp plastic bags of garlic and gungo peas. Piano fingers press into plums, tomatoes, and soursops. Family trains weave through renk side streets. Sale medleys boom — *yuh want a good wash out buy di prune and peppermint bush fi di gas*; clashing with street Pastors, *God a come fi him world yuh see, yuh betta repent*. Mommy and I eavesdrop on Trisha's eviction trial and Delroy's bun-giving. Market women make-shift cardboard beds for toddlers. Older daughters braid hair; sons hijack trollies to sell soft drinks, cash notes wrap knuckles like bandages; fathers drive handcarts with spliffs hanging off lips, *coconut fi wash off yuh heart*. Gold teeth men inspect likkle girls, *psst brownin, empress, cutie, fifty dolla a pound fi di pumpkin weh sweet like yuh*. Barefoot yutes sneak off with loose mangoes and naseberries, vendors too old to chase, *mi will obeah unnu*. Transactions end with blessings every time, except when customers ask, *tek off likkle something nuh*. Police jeeps patrol with long guns eager to fill cupboards at home.

Classifieds: Brute Neighbour

FOR SALE

Family home in coveted community.
4 Bed & 4 ½ Bath with soaring ceilings,
open-air kitchen and dining, boundless
lounge, a helper's quarter, carport,
veranda and a private backyard
with scrumptious fruit trees. Plus
brute neighbour.

SOLD

Every after-school, my sister's bare hands
juiced fruits while me and my half-
dressed dolls strewn across the veranda.
Our rottweiler chased and ragged our
house clothes, nipped at our bottoms
like oxtail bones.

BICYCLE WANTED

The brute's heist successful. Our rhinestone
bicycles, wheelless; handlebars melted
and sculpted into mango tree ornaments.

COFFIN NEEDED

Underneath his favourite rose bush,
our rottweiler dead, next to rat poison
grains. Our first funeral.

SUPERNATURAL POWER NEEDED

At night, her buckets fetched water
from our pipes to hydrate her hoodoo
garden. She pleasured an Obeah man;
left my sister frantic, *mi a see duppy,
mi a guh kill myself.* Mama delivered
her to a therapist, then a priest prayed
and cleansed her in lime and saltwater.

BRICK LAYER

Weed butts, tea bags and chicken fat,
hurled through our bedroom windows. The
brute's smell shadowed us in our sleep
when she slapped her wet clotty rawness
onto our white wall, we woke to red brick.

SECURITY NEEDED

Mommy drove my sister and I home
from school. Before she handed us over to
our helper, the brute's gunman smashed
our car window. All eyes stared at the
barrel. Mama bawled out *gunman, gunman
Maureen nuh come out fi di pickney dem.*
The mercy of God redirected bullets.
The brute perched over the wall and
cackled, *gyal and pickney fi dead.*

FOR RENT

Family home in coveted community.
4 Bed & 4 ½ Bath with soaring ceilings,
open-air kitchen and dining, boundless
lounge, a helper's quarter, carport,
veranda and a private backyard
with scrumptious fruit trees. Plus
brute neighbour.

CONFESSIONAL BOOTH WANTED

The brute's brother repented on her behalf,
boi *Miss Eva, mi sorry. Yuh nuh do mi sista
nothin, mi nuh know why she tek set pon yuh
suh.* Reasons ran around like cockroaches weh
hard fi kill, Mama's garment factory and
printery, her husband and new van. If she
di wutless dem woulda be best of friends.

Inna Di Trenches

Bellies bawl out like mongrels
but hot gyal nuh walk a street
and beg. Madda drives yutes round
wid gas tank swirling droplets like beer keg—
searching for nine-night with no guest list,
serving meaty mannish water and steamed fish.

Before school runs, Madda creeps out to rough up
ATMs, tears grease debit cards, empty hands
send slack jaw yutes to breakfast clubs for ackee,
dumpling and tea.

At dinner time, she scouts supermarket aisles,
yuh did know seh wata bill coulda wrap bully beef,
and pockets can tun measuring cup fulla flour?

Yutes empty Madda's money stash pot
while landlord's bolt cutter hands vanish padlocks.
Bedtime reach dem inna di parking lot.
Madda and yutes interlock like Tetris blocks
pon di backseat. Madda seh, *yutes haffi eat,*
even if there must be a kneeling.

Tief like Puss

The eviction notice hang like panty on a clothesline. Hands grab,
scrunch and tucks it into brassiere. Your mother's
pride is a cracked peg under the landlord's feet.
Outside your 'old home', in the car, you both play tic-tac-toe
in the *Classifieds* section of the newspaper.

Viewings: all roads that gulp gas and never lead home.
Yet, in the eleventh hour, a faultless apartment appears.
Two women, all smiles, welcome you into a space
that isn't theirs, but you do not know this yet.

There is silence throughout your tour, no warrior neighbours;
only bakers who gift fresh batches. Your fingers roam
across luxurious art frames and furniture, fantasising
about future sleepovers. Your inner child hulking in the living room.
The women pat you on the head and say, *you can have it all,*
excluding the poodle, pay today, keys tomorrow.

You say, 'this is crazy' as in an outlandish miracle,
your mother says, *this is funny*, as in off, but her noes are exhausted.
You can't help but remember how their tongues slit
the lining of your mother's purse, emptying her last.

This is the first time you see your mother surrender
her commotion. No searching for mercy, not a *Jesus Christ*
nor *Bomborassclat* just shrugging shoulders and siren sighs.

The house claims several families in one day.

When Yuh Point Finga, Three Point Back

after Hanif Abdurraqib

           Maddas ah di only ones weh remember dem
           sons inna three months' time.

Mosquito bullets zip through windows
from untrained militants weh escape
through zinced-up alleyways like rats.

           Politicians smackdown Dancehall artists weh
           sing massacres, *bwoy ah choke inna blood,*
           body stiff like it ah float inna flood.

Dancehall artists protest officers
weh unplug sound systems mid-wine
cah bribe envelope tuck too neat inna pocket.

           Officers seh parliament is a fish market.
           Garrison leaders and politicians walk inna
           lockstep stuffing ballot boxes like spice buns.

Granny *seh, Jamaica deh inna doldrums from mi
madda's time.* Blame begins not where the stray
bullet darts from.

If Wi Neva Block Di Road, Wi Wouldn't Find Her

Mi know sumn di off when mi come home fi see di rice neva wash.

Rusty fridge, wild bushes and waste tyres dash pon another shallow ditch.
From doo-doo plaits to relaxed hair, my little girl turns house keys
into knuckle rings for her walks home. Before passing a pack

of alleyway yutes, she lowers her uniform skirt enough to sweep the ground.
Young [redacted], otherwise called [redacted], did not return home.
The officer's baton knocks on the front door to notify me.

Fahda God, why dem dweet? He suspects that she is just another force-ripe
plantain: girls like that officers wait for the peeled skin tossing
before detaining fruit flies responsible for the attack.

Officers only tie up hands like bread bag when night breeze graze pumpum
in the wee hours. You fortunate mothers, shop for fitted crocus bags
when your girl's guineps turn breadfruits, thank God, fi di likkle mercies.

Community Breeds Miracle

CCTV 10/09/21 20:00: [skipping raisin bread and cheese]
CCTV 10/09/21 20:01: [walking knife and rope]
CCTV 10/09/21 20:02: [a vanishing act]

Three nights, mosquitoes sip from me as my belly quietens field crickets.
Mama—*wah dis Fahda God? Mi jus send her guh a shop fi di likkle tings.*
Daddy— *even if yuh   her, send her home.*

Courtyard roosters send for two hundred mesh marinas, jeans shorts
        and flip-flops.
Voices belong to the cutlasses, *funeral parlour a wait fi yuh bwoy.*
I emerge a muddy dolly.

Luck scratches the community's palms.
Two hundred buy *Cash Pot* lottery tickets,
3 (*dead*), 16 (*young girl*) and 27 (*big fire*).

He bolts through brushes, while fire gobbles up his home;
girlfriend flees panties and document free.
He interrupts clinking *Red Stripe* bottles

snatches the neck of another young girl like me.
He drags pink ribbons into a vegetated area;
shrubs pinch hair like her mother's braiding technique.

Two hundred sore throats and weary flip-flops hunt again.
Out of the pit, she drapes over her uncle's shoulder.
Community bows, *wi glad wi get di girls dem, but a him wi di want.*

Shhh... Gunshot Can Pick Padlock

for Isheka

Boney rastaman strings guitar
sings to his empress with yellow-corn

gapped teeth while she stirs ital stew. She forgets
to make his favourite homemade lemonade.

He ransacks home.
Aye gyal yuh know me?

He drags her body outside like a mic stand.
Whacks gun across her forehead and his

like drum skin. Her sunken collarbone
a washbowl collecting blood that drips

from her temple. His teeth sink into her shoulders.
Mute neighbours lurk behind pinched curtains.

He spotlights them, u*nnu want a show, seh bet
mi shoot her*. Neighbours return to washing

panties, hair and dishes. Free tour tickets slip
underneath their doors before the nightly news.

Tomorrow, neighbours will kekeke with him.
His empress will sweep their veranda

with a gentle hum, her smile will bleed
sunshine. When he's away, the elders

will hold her face in tenderness and whisper
If yuh nuh want to be pocketable for the sky,

when him start wid him foolishness
yuh fi boil di honey and pour it inna him work shoes,

crush laxatives like ginga and sprinkle it ova him ital stew,
mix di scotch bonnet pepper and lime juice and dash it inna him eye.

Snapper

for Kemesha, Kimanda, Sharalee, Rafaella and Kishawn

Father's Day reminds Kemesha of her daddy's brown-stew fish.
Gratitude rings his phone for the recipe.

He begins, alright tell mi when yuh ready. Method:
1) Wash di fish wid lime and vinegar.
2) Rub dem dung wid salt and black pepper.
3) Dash in yuh scotch bonnet, garlic and bell pepper inna hot oil.
4) Chuck in di fish fi fry, den dash weh di oil.
5) Add likkle wata and browning, den put di pot fi simma fi ten minutes.

Two days later, Kemesha and her fifteen-, twelve-, five- and two-year-old
leak like half-open ketchup bottles. Outside, a hundred crow residents
sit on rooftops waiting for the white sheets and stretchers. Phones film.
Soldier boys weep into masks, setting barricade tape.
Half-empty parliament offers one-minute silence.
Friends egg each other on, *dat deh bwoy wicked. Him fi get mince up.*

Her mother's joy burns, *di bwoy weh we feed, massacre*
mi only daughter and grandchildren. Her father's reality
inedible, *yuh hear bout these things but never think—*
Five gone. Mi wonda if she did cook di fish
fi di murda bwoy.

Water Polo Sessions Before Coke

Classmates pile into taxis. Conductors bawl out *onemore-onemore, everybody can hold, unnu lap up man.* You doodle on the school gate until your driver cruises through with a smouldering patty on the front seat. You and your boy fling yourselves into the backseat, holding hands inside an unzipped backpack. On the other side of your window, shirtless cocoa-head yutes with tarmac soles, pop-lock under traffic lights. In their hands, a bottle of soap water and a windscreen squeegee. On the sidewalk, their mother perches on a white bucket breastfeeding. Your boy has a traffic light family. He works weekends because of water polo practice. You both arrive, the smell of chlorine welcomes you. During warm-up, your boy swims behind you for the view then speeds up to squeeze your bottom on the glide through. He breathes, and you breathe, never running out of breath. Underwater there are only kisses. No tears. After training you both jump off the highest diving board holding hands. Two bullets darting through water. We play Marco Polo, I say 'Marco' he replies, alive. *Polo.*

Extradition of Drug Lord Dudus Coke:
Barbican Girl Dash Weh Tivoli Boy

Dudus / breath-taker of dutty yutes / preying on likkle girls'
cellphones and chochos / he pretzels politicians' arms / so fathers
can tief light to keep stoves on / his cash lines the bras of single
mothers / who send their sons to your school / with their A*s /
waves and clarks shoes /

prime minister bruce golding / approves Dudus' extradition /
your principal's intercom interrupts lunchtime / year group
becomes a herd of whispers / shuffling to collect bags / ears cock
for loose lips on staff walkie talkies / everyone sprints to their
drivers / your boy / shoves himself into a tivoli chi-chi bus /
that mounts sidewalks to get him home / while / your barbican
prado / cruises to water polo training

at training / with every other stroke you glance at the plumes of
smoke / in the distance / coming from tivoli / police helicopters
chopping your coach's commands / you have three missed calls
from your boy / you listen to his voicemail when you get home /
he says *jah know mi nuh know if me and mi family dem a guh mek
it / if mi dead / and dem seh mi did shoot afta di police / a lie dem
a tell /*

meanwhile / in the name of President Dudus / tivoli gunmen
buss shot after shot / not even a spot check for granny-less
verandas / scrap vehicles and gas cylinders block cherry stain
streets / your boy's eardrums grind like pimento / his little sister
and brother's squeals stow in their kitchen cupboards / from his
bedroom window he prees three of his bredrins plead the blood of
jesus as they sit in their own / pooling / while rumours have it /
underground / Dudus is a sewer rat / wearing a stiff wig for
disguise

the next day / prime minister calls a state of emergency for tivoli
/ you neither adjust / nor die / but your boy vanishes / for a
while / you ramp next to his empty desk / ask about his
whereabouts / but not enough / in the tivoli community /
mothers are graduating from sniffing foreheads / green armpits /
to heaving at compost flesh / top lips marrying snotty nose-tips /
single beds / open caskets

The Morning after the Extradition of Drug Lord Dudus Coke

Bed and fridge frames guard zinc houses'
ashes. Militant boots inspect streets

like fowls to arrest the living. Pockets
empty of zip ties after hogtying the

dead. In tower estates, the rotting scent
of pigs, dogs and humans smoke out

the living. Snipers on alert for desperate
nostrils. Relatives duck and dive

from bullets to retrieve their dead.
Corpses are children again, only instead

of being thrown into piles of fresh
laundry. they plop on top of the rubbish

on street corners. Outside Tivoli Garden's
Community Centre, toddlers play

scrimmage football as officers match
hole-filled bodies to mothers reaching into

bras for photos of their sons; the back
listing scars, tattoos and birthmark

locations for pathologists. Mother says
I lost [   ], my son, in di incident,

I need to find him. The officer says,
be patient mama, your quivering time

will come. Another mother says *a mi*
get mi son inna dis, mi shoulda leave

politics alone, mi pickney wouldn't dead,
nuhbody nah get my vote again,

when mi bury him, mi a move.
Funerals range from open

to closed to
no casket.

Puss and Dog Nuh Have Di Same Luck

My brothers' bodies are shell holders
for bullets, I escape staring into the barrel.
My bulletproof vest is the US/Mexico border.
Birthing two girls makes me willing
to fold our bodies like garments to stuff a barrel.

Midway to becoming US residents, I call mama,
with an unclear voice as if speaking while gargling water,
~~Unnu can stop pray now,~~
~~wi reach, thank yuh Fahda God.~~
I am an inmate and
only two of us are alive.

My five-year-old is a nameless doll floating
somewhere out there. I remember clutching
my bible while walking past bones;
no water nor spit left to drink;
so hungry, cacti consume our stomachs.

I can't remember
my last glimpse of Cami, just the running,
the guard dogs, dirt bikes and helicopter hunting us.
I carry that river in my eyes, every day.
Now, Cami lives in two places at once,
spirit by the Colorado River; body resting in Jamaica.

The Path of No Papers

To ward off separation, tears nuh fi water dung cereal,
catch di school bus, lips fi ziplock-shut, find di pickney
dem weh look and act like prospectus kids.

Remember, mi womb neva birth nuh clown, nuh play
wid mi. Answer di teacher's questions, but nuh tell dem,
mi business, know when fi kibba yuh mouth.

Nuh guh to di school nurse, even if yuh haffi squeeze
yuh batty jaws tight like yuh a try wring out panty.
Rum, turmeric, ginger, lemon and honey deh home.

Yuh have a bed fi liddung inna?
Yuh love people yard too much.
Mi yard a nuh amusement park?
Di answer is no.

Every time yuh leave di yard reach fi di holy oil,
dem fi can fry plantain pon yuh forehead.
Blood like fi stain hoodies, sagging jeans, and gang colours.

Nuh mek yuh granny tongue talk fi yuh outta road,
twist up yuh tongue and twang. Rip off yuh fahda name
and staple a white one before yuh touch di keyboard.

If yuh eye see nuttin, juke dem out, neva call di squaddie dem.
Dis a how wi mek sure dem nuh separate wi.
Cyah seh mi neva warn yuh seh yuh nuh have papers.

If all a dis nuh work, and yuh / wi get deported,
nuh worry, a nuh your fault.

Babylon Wah Tun Us Inna Rasta Mouse

Step inna one dance fi hold a medz
and di MC bawl out *Jah, Rastafari,*
praise to di most high, Selesai.
Before him, a sea of tweed caps clutch locks,
button-down linen shirts flaunt chest hairs and gold chains.
This cramped garage: sanctuary for slow sways, prayerful eyes,
and ganja. Okra tongues provoke boasy bwoy's peace,
he backs out cutlass like a handkerchief.
MC *seh, nuh war to wi ting, just love and unity*
and di Irie vibes carry on.

Blonde neighbour summons her pack
and bawls Jesus off di cross
like seh lions a prowl through di sound system.
Babylon's batons bash doors their speaky-spokey accents,
turn off this racket.
Ras dem disperse like mad ants,
some faces get ketch under Babylon's boots,
speaky-spokey accents say go back to your country.
If flatten bodies on concrete coulda mek a boat
Babylons' spit woulda send dem sailing home, long time.

Motherland Nuh Wah Wi Again

Rebuild Rebuild Rebuild
Unnu hear weh di Queen of England seh?
She seh, mi fi come wid mi whole fambily.
My stush stride follows four hundred to board the ship. I wave
goodbye to gulley pools and low-hanging meals. My yute doodles
postcards by my feet.
Home: a cherry seed.

HMT *Empire Windrush* docks in Essex.
Spit and slurs unwelcome me. My Black nurse face a toilet bowl
for white folks' bedpans; my husband a cleaner dodging Molotov
cocktails.

Leave Leave Leave

Unnu hear weh di Prime Minister seh?
She seh, mi fi guh back a mi yard, and tek mi whole fambily.
The Home Office's charter flight to Jamaica
is the first time I rebuke freeness.

Muscle memory goes back thirty years
my face pressed to the window as the plane lands. ~~Strangers~~
Relatives collect me and tour me around the housing scheme. I pit
stop to grin at old faces
that yell *Pinkie, you dat? Welcome home gyal.*

Restore Restore Restore

In bed, I toss and turn thinking about tomorrow.
Must go to:
    The Registrar General's Department fi di birth certificate
    Tax Administration Jamaica fi di Taxpayer Registration Number
    Supermarket fi di toothbrush, panty, and deodorant.

Cardi B Meets My Green Card Interview

'Pop up, guess who, bitch?' Outside the embassy
the line and forms are endless. In the waiting room,
my pen taps accompany the hum of the water cooler.
The interviewer calls my name and a stiff polite smile
follows him into his cubicle.

Interviewer: *Be honest as possible.*

Me: 'only real ish comes out my mouth; right hand to Jesus.'

What is your name?

'I'm the hottest in the street, know you prolly heard of me.'

Do you have any siblings?

'Look, my bitches all bad, my niggas all real.'

Religious practice?

'I wear off-white at church, prolly make the preacher sweat,
read the Bible, Jesus wept.'

Have you ever committed any crimes?

'You a goofy, you an opp.'

Why do you want to move to the US?

'What's mine is yours; I don't understand; honestly, don't give a heck
'bout who ain't fond of me; I like proving folks wrong, I do what
they say I can't.'

What will you do once you move to the US?

'Let's find out and see, make money moves, what bitch working
as hard as me?'

ACKNOWLEDGEMENTS

To God be the glory. Grateful for his grace, mercy and favour in writing this book.

Highly grateful to my parents and family. Thank you for all your sacrifices and support.

Special thanks to Tolu Agbelusi, you have been the ultimate champion, truly a God-ordained mentor, thank you for your wisdom, and generosity. You were often a motivator when I didn't know which way was up.

To the elders who took the time to grace me with their energy and knowledge, I am highly grateful: Vanessa Kisuule, Raymond Antrobus, Cecilia Knapp, Bridget Minamore, Malika Booker, Nick Makoha, Roger Robinson, Ajanae Dawkins, Jacob Sam-La Rose, Lionheart, Toby Campion and Rachel Long.

Thank you to all my outstanding poetry peers who I've met on various emerging writers' programmes. I am beyond grateful that you all graced me with your intelligence, talent, support, time, energy, compassion and grace. May you all continue to experience overflow in all aspects of your life. Special thanks to Obsidian Group C and E, Griots Well Squad, Unislam and CUPSI squad, Lola, Oaks, TG, NJ, Fathima, Fahad, and Kate.

Thank you to my church community, your prayers have assisted this book's transition from Prayer Request to Praise Report.

Grateful for the collectives and institutions that provided me with a space to write and learn: Roundhouse Poetry

Collective, Barbican Young Poets, Griots Well, the London Library Emerging Writers Programme, Obsidian Foundation, Writerz and Scribz, Apples and Snakes, BBC *Words First*, Young Identity, Uni Slam, Malika's Poetry Kitchen and UKNA.

Grateful to those who have published my work: *The White Review, Magma Poetry, Bad Betty Press, Stand Magazine, Poetry Review, Bath Magg, Poetry Birmingham Literary Journal, Lumiere Review, Anamot Press, Poetry Wales, Mslexia, Propel Magazine, Ink Sweat and Tears, Anthropocene, The Adriatic Magazine, Re.creation,* and Peekash Press.

Thank you to the following competitions that have placed my work, *Mslexia* Women's Poetry Pamphlet Prize, *The White Review* Poet's Prize, *The Rialto* Nature and Place Competition, Bridport Prize, Bridport Young Writers Award, *Poetry Wales* Pamphlet Competition, Oxford Brookes International Poetry Competition, and the Rebecca Swift Women's Poets Prize, and to the Society of Authors for an Eric Gregory Award.

A massive thank you to Arts Council England for my DYCP funding which allowed me to have the time to write and the ability to have mentors throughout the process of writing this book.

Lastly, thank you to Imtiaz Dharker, the *Mslexia* team, the Bloodaxe Books team and Neil Astley for all their efforts.

Courtney Conrad is a Jamaican poet who now lives in London. Her debut pamphlet *I Am Evidence* (Bloodaxe Books/Mslexia, 2023) was the winner of the 2022 *Mslexia* Women's Poetry Pamphlet Competition judged by Imtiaz Dharker, and includes some work which won her an Eric Gregory Award in 2022. She received a Bridport Prize Young Writer Award in 2021. She was shortlisted for *The White Review* Poet's Prize, the Manchester Poetry Prize, Oxford Brookes International Poetry Competition and *Aesthetica* Creative Writing Award's Poetry Prize, and was longlisted for the National Poetry Competition. Her poems have appeared in *Magma Poetry, The White Review, Poetry Review, Bath Magg* and *Poetry Birmingham Literary Journal.* She is an alumna of the London Library Emerging Writers Programme, MPK, Obsidian, Griots Well Collective, Roundhouse Poetry Collective, and Barbican Young Poets.